Peter's World

By Hugh R. Clinton III

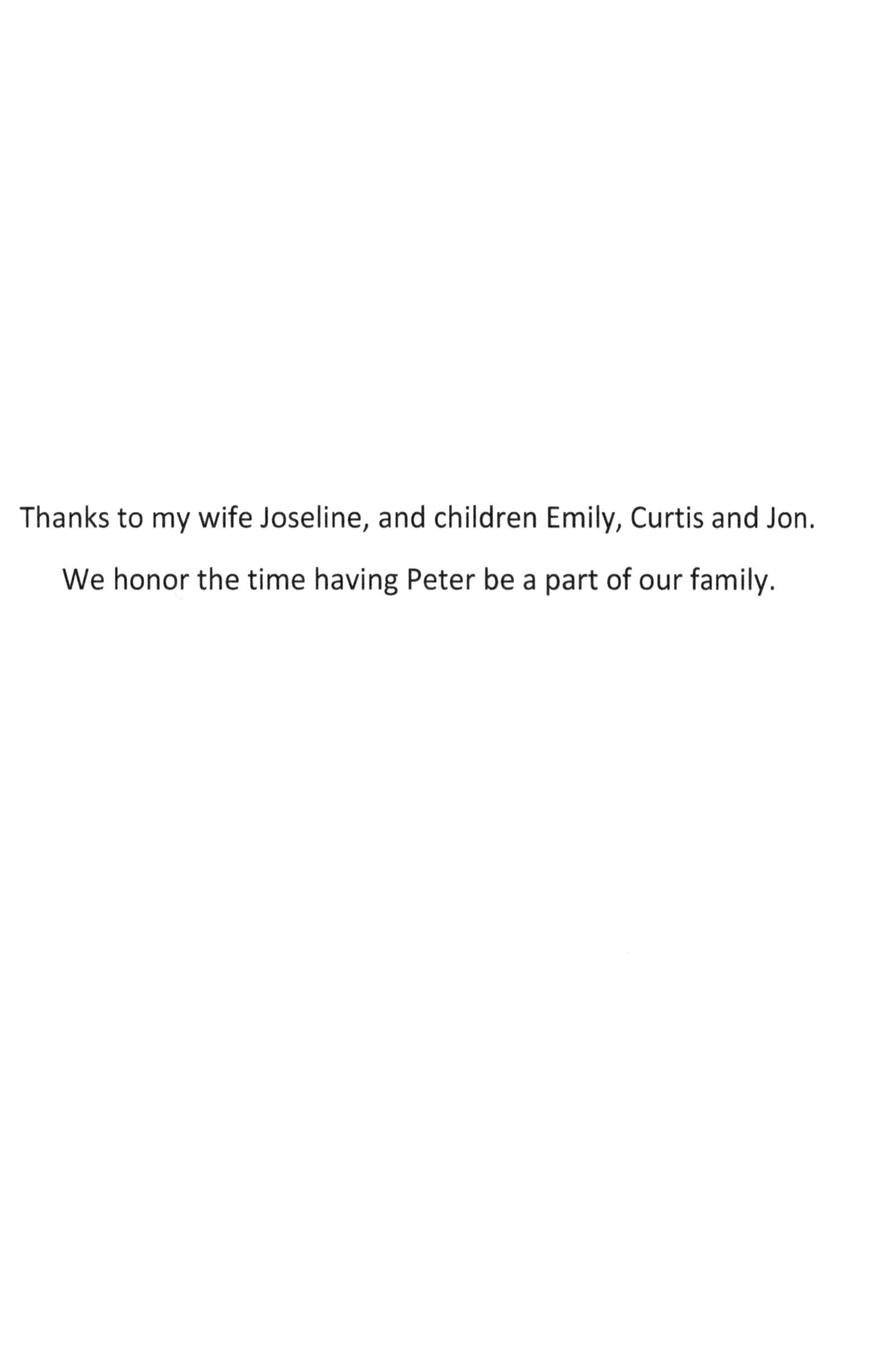

Thanks to my wife Joseline, and children Emily, Curtis and Jon.

We honor the time having Peter be a part of our family.

On a cold February day Peter joined a family.
Two weeks prior he was taken from his family and placed in a pet store.
Now Peter is in a new home.

In his new home, he looks around at his surroundings.
This was not like his old home.

He checks everything out in his room.
Sniffing as he goes exploring his environment and new space.

Checking and more checking.

He looks at other rooms.

Listening to the sounds around him.

Some days Peter listened to one of the kids playing their saxophone.

Every morning he eats his piece of kale.
He loves his vegetables.

Peter can do tricks. The kids would show Peter a piece of banana and say "spin Peter, spin". As a reward for spinning in a circle, he is given the banana.

Taking a break, he likes the morning sun coming through the front window.

At lunch he has his blueberries.

He loves his sweet blueberries.

Peter sits looking at the front door.

The bus will come, and the kids would be home from school.

With the kids home, he is given a slice of apple, thereby getting a nutritious fruit. Vitamins to help keep him healthy.

To keep his teeth clean and trimmed, he chews on a piece of cherry hardwood.

Resting, he takes the form like a chicken sitting on an egg.

This is Peter's favorite position on his floor.

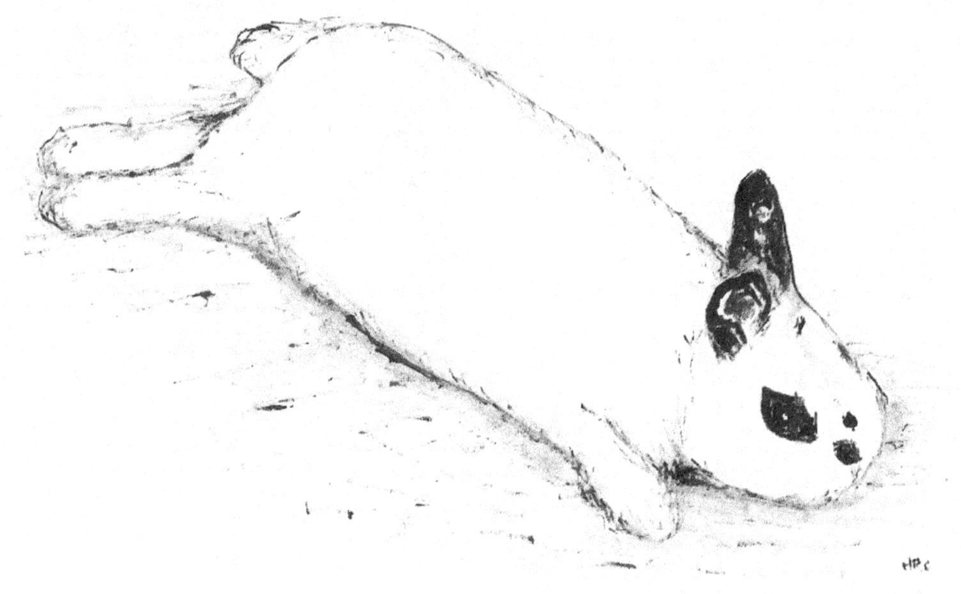

Peter, with his head down, likes basking in the late afternoon sun shining through the back door window.

Peter stands on his hind feet and looks out the window.
He wants to know if any friends are around.

Before going to bed, he has an evening snack with a leaf of romaine lettuce.

Seeing the kids getting ready for bed, it is bedtime for Peter.
Another great day.
But tomorrow is special.

Today is Peter's birthday.

Peter celebrates with a party hat, a piece of carrot, and cake for his family.

Another great day in Peter's world.